AMELIA THE
INVENTOR EXTRAORDINAIRE

Written by
J. W. Kohler

Illustrated by
Kate Fallahee

This is a work of fiction. Names, characters, places, and incidents either are the product of the author's imagination or are used fictitiously. Any resemblance to actual persons, living or dead, events, or locales is entirely coincidental.

Copyright © 2020 by J.W. Kohler

All rights reserved. No part of this book may be reproduced or used in any manner without written permission of the copyright owner except for the use of quotations in a book review.

Publishing quality books loved by children and adults alike.

www.developingmindspublishing.com

This book is dedicated to Jemma, Mia, and Jess.
Continue to imagine big and never give up.

Though she hadn't yet come up with a successful invention, there are still lots of items she can notably mention.

Like a shirt made from salami, or a telephone that doesn't ring;

a toothbrush for your toes,
a vacuum for your nose,
or some greenish slimy thing.

Amelia was full of ideas and every morning, shortly after she awoke,

she would head to her workshop,
idea in her head beginning to prod and poke.

An inventor's job was never boring or dull;
in fact, it was fun and exciting.
Each day Amelia came up with new ideas,

like shorts with dimmable lighting.

One day, Amelia was visited by Winston the rat, who came from a neighboring town. He sported a top hat, wore a greenish cape, and held a cane that was dark brown.

"Why, hi there!" said Winston. "How do you do?
I wonder if you can make me an invention.
For I'm in need of some help, some help with my cane.
Of course, I will pay, did I mention?

At my age, I need a cane to walk,
but it often gets stuck, you see...
in holes, in roots, all sorts of things,
when I go to my home in the tree."

"I can help!" said Amelia, full of excitement, happy to help another creature. She began to think of a brand-new cane, one with a built-in rocket feature.

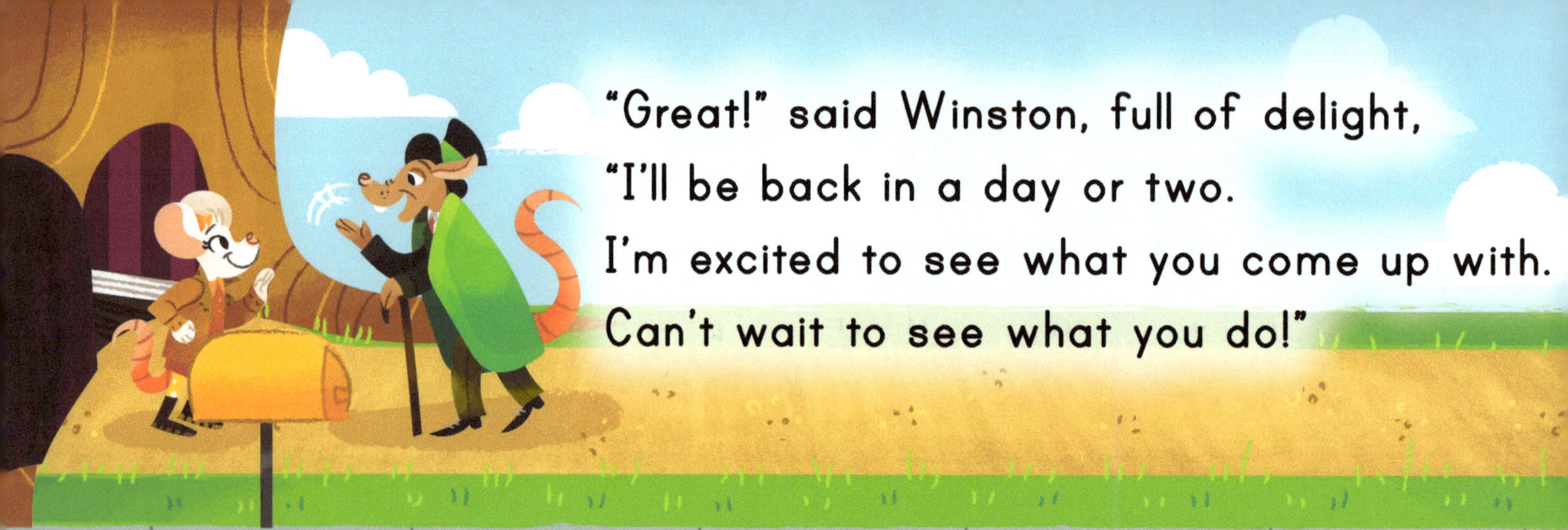

"Great!" said Winston, full of delight,
"I'll be back in a day or two.
I'm excited to see what you come up with.
Can't wait to see what you do!"

As soon as he left, Amelia started her project, her head full of thoughts.

To the cane she added rocket fuel,
a string, and tied two little knots.

"Here it goes!" she said as she lit the string, and the cane shot into the sky. And then for a moment, as brief as it was, into the air the cane did fly.

But after that moment, the cane changed directions and she heard a crashing sound,

CRASH!

as the cane broke into one hundred pieces, shattering as it hit the ground.

Was Amelia discouraged, distraught, or upset? Not even a little bit.

For Amelia knew it was never a failure, just a lesson to learn from it.

Next Amelia thought, "I need something less powerful," and ideas started to churn. "I got it!" said Amelia, for it was time for the bouncy cane to have its turn.

Amelia attached an old mattress spring, and then decided maybe one more.

Then she thought, "I'll add another to the cane, and just in case, another four!"

It was time. The cane was ready,
and Amelia gave it a test.
And bounce that cane did do,
and the extra springs gave it zest.

BOUNCE!

But maybe she had added just a bit too much spring. Maybe a bit too much might. For that cane kept bouncing down the road, and soon bounced right out of sight.

But was Amelia discouraged, distraught, or upset?

"I did it!" Amelia cried as she held up her proudest invention of all.

This time, the cane had a sword on one end, in case a pirate's capture should ye fall.

And just then, who should Amelia see, strolling back down the lane, but Winston the rat coming back to the workshop ready to pick up his cane.

"Well, hello there!" Winston said.
"I can't wait to see what you've created!"

Amelia held out the cane to show it to Winston, perfectly elated.

Winston took a good long look at the cane and decided to give it a try. But as Winston pushed the cane down, it stuck tight in the ground, and he let out a sigh.

"What do you think?" cried Amelia. "A cane with a sword! Don't you think it's grand? You will be able to fight off any swashbuckling pirates, whether it be on sea or land!"

"Well, Amelia," said Winston, "fighting off pirates I likely won't be, for I just need a cane that won't get stuck as I go to my home in the tree."

"Well, why didn't you say so?" Amelia asked, beaming with delight.

"You don't need a cane with rockets, or bounce, or one for a swashbuckling fight."

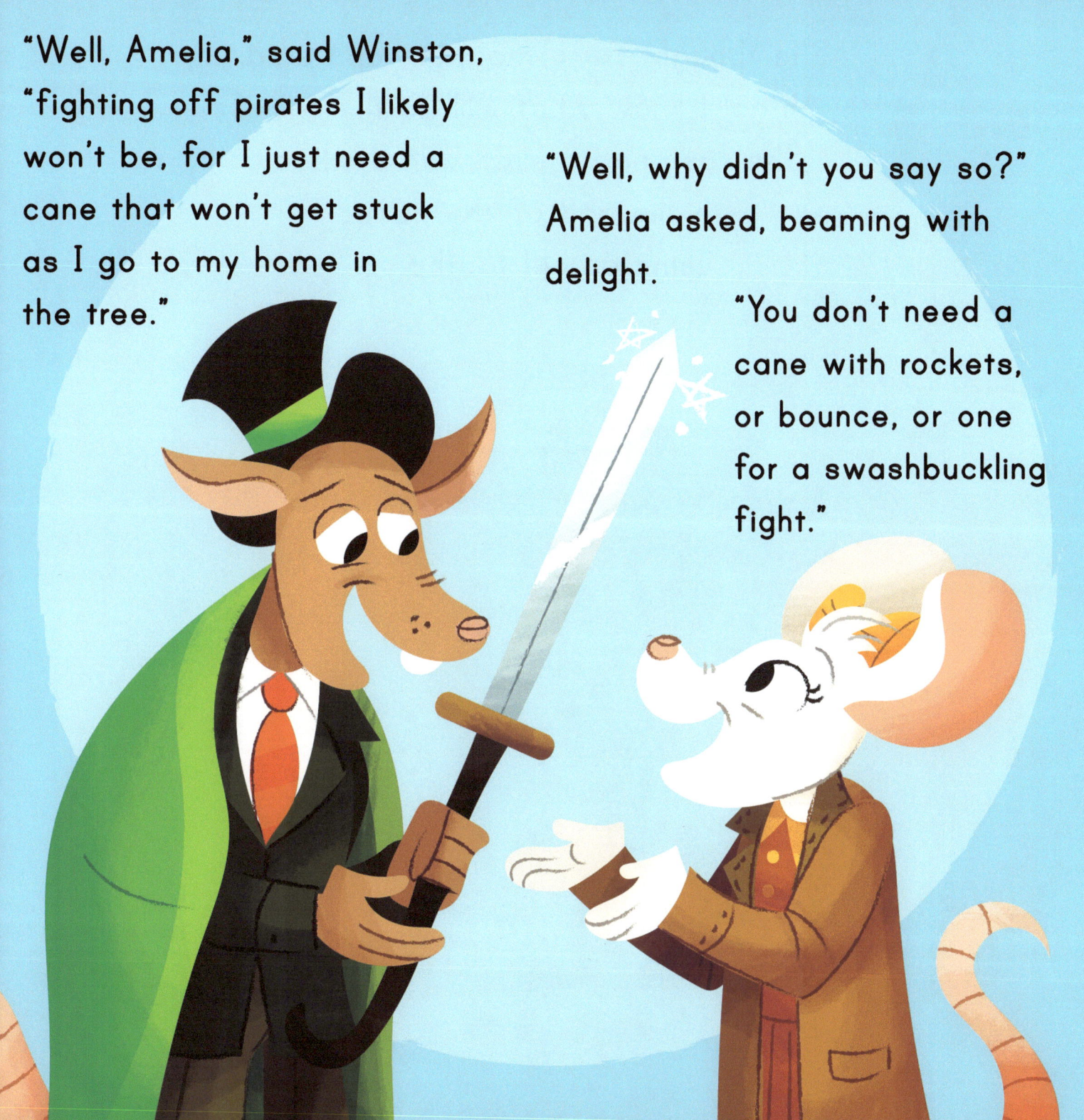

She thought for a moment, and said,
"Ah ha! I know what will do the trick!"
She fastened a skateboard wheel
to the end of the cane,
using an old toothpick.

When she was done, she handed the cane back and said, "Go on, give it a try! Go on, Winston! Tell me how it is! Come on now, don't be shy!"

Winston took the cane and went for a short stroll, testing it along the way.

He came back, a big smile on his face, and said, "Amelia, you made my day!

The wheel on the end is a perfect invention and smoothly drove down the road.

It didn't get stuck in holes, it went over roots, and it even helped lighten the load!"

"Glad to help!" Amelia replied,
"For an inventor's job is never through!
And should you need firepower,
like an engine or rockets, I know just what to do!"

"This should be fine for now," Winston replied, "Thanks again! Toodle-oo!"

And Amelia soon started helping many more mammals, and even some reptiles too.

For Amelia never got discouraged, distraught, or upset. Not even a little bit.

Amelia knew there is no such thing as a failure, just a lesson to learn from it.

CPSIA information can be obtained
at www.ICGtesting.com
Printed in the USA
LVHW070221290920
667382LV00013B/1870